C000063695

KELLY MARKS

HANDLING THE UNTOUCHED HORSE

J. A. ALLEN · LONDON

INTELLIGENT ⁂ HORSEMANSHIP

For information on **INTELLIGENT HORSEMANSHIP** and
Kelly Marks courses, demonstrations and merchandise worldwide
see our web site: **www.intelligenthorsemanship.co.uk** or write to
Intelligent Horsemanship, Lethornes, Lambourn, Berkshire RG17 8QS.
Telephone (+44) 01488 71300 or fax (+44) 01488 73783

Also available in this series:

Creating a Bond With Your Horse (ISBN 0 85131 795 2)

Leading and Loading (ISBN 0 85131 796 0)

Catching Horses Made Easy (ISBN 0 85131 840 1)

ACKNOWLEDGEMENTS

Thanks to Sandy Vandenberghe for lending me her untouched yearling
Hartsop Antics. All the photographs in the main text are taken within his
first hour of handling. Many thanks to my former students, now great
friends and associates, for their help and advice, especially Nicole Golding
on the literary side and Julia Scholes for her wonderful design for the
Intelligent Horsemanship logo. Thanks to Ian Vandenberghe, Linda Ruffle,
Dido Fisher, Jane Young and Brenda Whelehan for their constant support
and also Jess Wallace and Jane Young for their excellent photographs.
Thanks to John Beaton who came up with the idea for these books and who
has guided me throughout. Finally enormous thanks are due to Monty
Roberts whose generosity and inspiration in putting me on the path to
Intelligent Horsemanship have been immeasurable.

CONTENTS

INTRODUCTION

There are few things more rewarding than meeting a lovely yet sceptical, untouched horse and over a period of maybe minutes, hours or days causing him to believe that human beings are not so bad after all… that in fact, it is even good to be near them! You might imagine that nowadays, in Britain at least, it would be rare to come across groups of totally untouched horses. Surprisingly though, a large proportion of the correspondence I receive is from people who need advice about horses that they cannot get near, never mind catch. These horses give every appearance of being terrified of them and the people have no idea of the best way to proceed. It is not surprising: after all, it is not something that is taught at the average riding school.

Many of the wild herds in Britain are bred by hill farmers who have never had the time available to get these horses in and to educate them for people to use. It is once these horses reach the age of three or four that the owner decides 'enough's enough' and gets them rounded up for market – where they will very often go for meat. I have excellent students all over the world who are working with horses in the ways I will describe in this book. Their great work in forming a relationship and then going on to educate these horses means they have a future and the chance of a better life. Of course, the education works both ways.

Handling the untouched horse has now become a subject very close to my heart. It wasn't always that way though. I haven't always been familiar with such horses. When I worked with racehorses they used to come to us for

> ### What is a 'wild' horse or pony?
>
> I use the term to mean any horse that is untouched by (sympathetic) human hands. These horses are actually 'feral' to use the more scientific term, meaning their ancestors were previously domesticated. Scientists usually refer to groups of untouched horses as being in 'bands' rather than 'herds'.

starting as yearlings. They had been hard fed since weaning, had already been groomed, worn rugs and bridles, travelled in a horsebox, been led around the sales paddock and taught to stand up for prospective buyers who would have stroked and petted them. I used to think that was what an unhandled horse was!

I had plenty to learn and there was no better place to do that than Willow Farm from where I run many of my courses. Willow Farm in Witney, Oxfordshire, is the home of one of the biggest breeders of driving horses in Britain. These horses (about 130 at the last count) are mostly Hackneys crossed with Welsh cobs. With so many horses being bred in large, open fields dotted around the county, their handling prior to arriving at the farm as weanlings (at around six months old) is minimal. They will never have had any human contact except possibly at the moment of their birth and only then if there was a delay in the delivery. They've been a wonderful learning opportunity!

CASE STUDIES

Martine

Since gaining so much experience on working with the 'natural horse', I have been regularly volunteered whenever there is a wild or 'untouchable' horse in the area that needs to be brought in. Several of these have been featured on television. One was a beautiful five-year-old chestnut mare by the name of Martine and she was my first big challenge. Martine's owner had been ill and never got round to catching her and she was sold with two others in her field at the age of five. The new owner had managed to chase the others into a horsebox, and brought them over to me, but it had entailed the horses walking over a concrete bridge, about ten feet (three metres) in width. Martine took one look at this and said 'You've got to be joking!'

It was not only necessary to remove her from the field for the practical purpose of taking her to her new home, but there were health welfare issues too. The new owner noticed her front hooves were split right up to the coronet band, and she had developed abscesses. She was getting footsore, and he was becoming increasingly worried about whether she had a future at all.

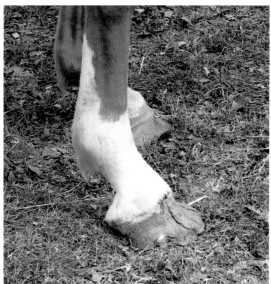

Martine the wild mare... maybe she was just put off by my taste in colours

Martine was named after the presenter who covered the dramatic story for television. Thankfully for all concerned it was a very happy ending with an additional programme put on showing me riding Martine and talking about her new home. Admittedly this was several months after I met this horse who when I first reached out to touch her jumped several feet in the air!

Bo

After becoming Oxfordshire's unofficial 'Wild Horse Catcher' I was approached by National Geographic to catch and work with a lovely, five-year-old, Welsh cob mare we named Bo for their 'Explorers Journal' television series. Bo had been brought up on the outskirts of London, not the first place you would think of as having many wild horses! When she was three years old they went to get her so that she could be transported to the Oxfordshire countryside. Unable to catch her, they chased her into the trailer. On her journey the floor of the trailer gave way and her hind leg went right through to the ground. Usually an accident like this is fatal but mercifully it happened when they were nearly at the destination and they managed to get her out with only the skin torn on the hind leg involved. Understandably she was even more sceptical about human involvement after this experience and had never allowed anyone near her again. Working to the type of plan I shall outline in this book, by the end of the day, she was not only caught… she was also being ridden!

above: Bo, the wild mare from National Geographic *below:* 'Ollie the Bad Tempered Foal'

Ollie

Another television horse was 'Ollie the Bad Tempered Foal' as he was dubbed by BBC 1's 'Barking Mad' research department. Ollie lived on the wild Welsh hills of Ammanford and sadly his mother died when he was just four months old. He was fortunate (or smart) enough to make his home in the garden of the Flynn family. The Flynns were very anxious to do whatever was best for Ollie but were at a loss as to how they should deal with this orphaned youngster. They made sure he had two feeds a day and tried to approach him gently but he repaid all their kindness by biting them and chasing them out of the garden! He was completely untouchable and they rang to ask if they could bring him to one of my demonstrations we were holding near them. 'But how can you get him to me?' I asked (this seemed a reasonable question in the circumstances). It turned out they had made Ollie a 'home' in a trailer. It was all comfortably made up with a straw bed and hay and Veronica Flynn would put a feed in there for him at 9.30am and 3.30pm (precisely) every day. Little Ollie was a bit of a prince as wild horses go – with the trailer being his palace. When the time came for him to come to the demonstration it was simply a question of timing things correctly so they only needed to close the ramp and away they went. A stroke of genius!

Of course, I don't just do horses for television! There are many other youngsters and untouched horses who have taught me an enormous amount about how to help them. What is more it seems the horses teach me something new every time. It is incredibly rewarding work to see a horse that was formerly terrified of human contact become a friend to human beings and, because of that, one always hopes, lead a better life.

Homebody or Wild Child... who has the better life?

This brings up an interesting subject. Are horses better off in the wild or in domesticity? In Britain today not many horses could get away without seeing human beings at some stage or another. Life is surely going to be a lot less stressful for them if they do not always regard humans as the enemy. I think it is fair to say that the best care and treatment in domesticity is surely better than the worst conditions of being in the wild but equally the reverse is true so we have a responsibility to provide our horses with the best that domesticity can offer. However, do not underestimate how harsh the wild can be. For those of you who are interested in the realities and statistics of horses living in the wild you would enjoy *Horses of the Wild Basin* by Joel Berger (University of Chicago Press). On the front cover three very attractive mares are photographed. Sadly, on the inside cover it reports that all three died that winter because of the extreme cold. Nature can be extremely hard.

Remember...

Hopefully, my experiences can now help you if you are preparing to start work with an untouched horse. At the very least I can offer suggestions that will make it very much safer for the pair of you. Of course, even though I try to set out suggestions and even 'rules', only you know the true situation. It is similar to having your first child. 'Experts' come out of the woodwork giving you all sorts of conflicting advice, but you need to remember that you are the one actually responsible for the horse or pony, you know your own ability and experience, the facilities you are working with and the time you have available in any given session. Each horse and situation can be different so you need to adapt as appropriate. Be wary of any advice that does not sound right to you – even mine! I'm here working at the computer drinking tea: I cannot see the full picture. I might say to you 'work with the horse in a small paddock' but if the only small paddock you have is made of barbed wire and the horse is terrified then that would be a disaster waiting to happen. Keep common sense and a sense of preservation for you and the horse to the fore at all times. If you would like more experienced assistance ring the Intelligent Horsemanship Association for help (the details are on page 2).

How to catch a wild horse

You first need to consider carefully the best way to go about this. Consider the facilities and helpers you have available. Give yourself the best chance to succeed by putting everything in your favour. Remember this is much fairer and less stressful on the horse as well. Also it is so much quicker this way. For instance, I have gone 'to all the trouble' on occasion of taking a round pen on a trailer to a field, setting it up and getting six friends to slowly encourage the horse into the round pen – the whole procedure taking about one hour from start to finish and being great fun and very rewarding. What a lot of effort you may say? And yet previous attempts at catching the horse had been taking place over years, yes I mean years, and people have just had a thoroughly frustrating time and maybe even injured horses or themselves in the process. Set it up right for yourself first time.

Separating the Horse

You need to find a way to separate the horse you intend to work with and get him on his own. It is virtually impossible to build up a relationship when he is in with a herd of other horses so you need to think in advance about how you are going to remove him from the others. If this is the case it may be that you need to catch the whole herd first and then separate him. In America they often used to round horses up into a corral shaped like a key-hole and made of brushwood and maybe post and rails as well. They would have a big open gateway that could be closed quickly so that the horses would not even realise they had been closed in. The corral would be circular in shape, meaning that the horses would be less likely to get trapped in corners and injure themselves or to break out.

My round pen is light and easily transportable on a trailer which is really handy, otherwise you just have to get innovative. You can drive the horses or horse into the pen from the back of another horse (what fun!) or people can slowly spread out behind the horses on foot and gently guide them into the pen. Do make sure you go very slowly and don't excite them, otherwise you will find them going off in all directions. Choose calm people to help you and plan out exactly what you're going to do and any contingency plans with your helpers beforehand.

Body Language

Your helpers all need to be proficient in body language. By this I mean they need to know that to send a horse away or push him back one should approach the horse squarely, with arms outstretched and moving them alternately up and down in a jerky way. At the same time one looks the horse directly in the eye. If they want a horse to come towards them or at least past them and not be intimidated, they need to look down, have their body at a forty-five degree angle to the horse with their arms by their sides and move very smoothly.

Alternative Strategies

Another good strategy for anyone who has a number of young horses is to have a little catchment field. It makes it very easy if the horses are used to being called in to be fed and closed in there regularly.

If it is only one horse that cannot be caught or at least if there are some easy horses in the group, a good way is to find out which is the

Following another horse into the pen

'lead mare'. This is usually the oldest mare in the group, or at least the one who has been out with the others the longest. Bring her in and the others will follow. It really works!

Dress for success

When working with the unhandled horse, I suggest you wear a hard hat. It not only prevents a painful knock to the head but it means you don't have to worry, say, if a horse is throwing his head around initially, and that helps you do a better job. Some horses learn to intimidate people by throwing their heads around and moving the person away. Another thing I find with unhandled horses is that they often like to sniff your face when you are close enough. I can allow them to do this because if I thought they might take a little nip I'd just dip my head away and let them get my hat.

I always wear gloves when working with ropes to protect my hands. Some people find this uncomfortable, but it is usually just a matter of getting used to them. Good, protective, non-slip footwear is a must. I would not choose a bright yellow or white jacket to approach a young horse! Neither would I want to approach an unknown horse in just a T-shirt. Unhandled horses will sometimes nip out of curiosity but it can still be painful! I find a waterproof wax jacket is quite lightweight yet protective. Be aware of how sensitive horses' senses are – particularly the more naturally they've been kept – do not wear perfume and keep deodorants lightweight – particularly with colts.

You now have to get your horse completely on his own. In the old days the cowboys used to just rope the horse they wanted and drag him out. There is an easier, safer way without even touching the horse. It is only a question of getting horses you don't want out through the gate, whilst keeping the horse you do want in. Separating a group of horses is a bit like separating egg yolks from the whites; there's a knack to it and it can be tricky and take several goes; but it can be done if you work at it!

The Working Area

Next you need to think about where you are going to work with the horse. Always work in a safe, enclosed area with a good surface i.e. not bare concrete. In the States and Australia round pens and 'yards' are the norm for the initial handling, leading and riding of young horses. More and more people in Britain are seeing the benefits of these, the most important aspect being the safety of horse and handler. Obviously if we are on foot we are going to need to work from a smallish area to start with if we are expecting to touch, or to get a rope on this horse. You may even work from a large stable, but it must be big enough for you to move around in, be well bedded down, have no potentially dangerous obstructions or protrusions, and be easy to get out of quickly if necessary.

Later on, when we do the first leading lessons with our horse we will still need to work in an enclosed area with a soft, safe surface. It is a big mistake to let a horse learn how much stronger he is than you! We can do this by always working in an enclosed area until we are quite sure he is safe to lead and understands the benefits of staying with us. We need to find a way to get our horse into that area. Again, it could be by gently

driving him or it could be by taking a lead horse to show him the way.

Remember...

1. **Horses don't learn when they're over-excited and distracted.** It is a good idea to let the horse acclimatise to his new area for a while. Make sure he is comfortable with hay and water and shade and then let him explore his new surroundings. He may cry for his companions for a while but he should settle down within an hour.

2. **Horses can become habituated to new experiences surprisingly quickly.** The less distracted and more settled the horse is the easier he is going to be to work with. It would be good if you could be by the pen or stable (reading this book!) or at least go over to him at every available opportunity to let him get used to you.

3. **Horses take note of who is supplying their food and water.** I have found a way that works well in acclimatising unhandled horses to humans is to put them into barn stabling where there is a lot of human activity going on. I go in to feed and water them at regular intervals but do not do any more than that in the first three or four days.

4. **Horses learn by observing their peers.** While the horses watch the others being handled and get to know that humans are going to provide them with food and water regularly it helps to put their minds at rest about what is going to happen to them. I have seen untouched horses change quite dramatically on occasion without any actual physical human contact at all.

5. **Horses have a strong need to bond.** Alternatively, if you are planning to work with your horse at the earliest opportunity there is also an

advantage in having him in an area where he cannot see other horses at all. You make up for the lack by visiting him with food regularly. Horses are naturally gregarious and feel the need for company. In the absence of other horses they are going to be far more willing to look to you as a possible companion.

6. It is possible to go too slowly as well as too fast. Regular amounts of time spent every day are really going to help.

Exploring the Options

If we put our truly wild horse straight into the round pen, we could accomplish the starting points of a 'Join Up' in less than twenty minutes or so (for more details on the system of Join Up do read *Creating a Bond With Your Horse* in this series). That is, he would start to face us when we stopped him in the pen. He might even take a step or two to follow us as we move away from him. If he is really wild and unhandled though, and has never been taught to lead or to be comfortable being touched, he is likely to run away again every time we get close enough to touch him, and this can go on for some time. The reason for this is that at this stage of his education, our touching him won't be a reward, it will be a punishment.

When Monty Roberts caught Shy Boy out in the wild, remember he had sixty-three years' experience of dealing with mustangs and he knew that mustangs are incredibly tough and hardy. Monty wanted to work with Shy Boy in the wild to show what it was possible to do. I do not imagine anyone is under the impression he was suggesting it was the most practical choice of method. Catching a completely unhandled horse can be done with Join Up but it is not

always the easiest way for the horse, particularly if the handler does not have the body language absolutely 'spot on'. If the horse has not learned the value of touch, he may only feel that it is a punishment to be touched so it could take hours, confusing the youngster, and possibly putting a strain on his limbs before they are ready. I have seen people who are not experienced with these types of youngsters do this, and very often the main thing that the youngster has been taught is innumerable different ways to avoid being caught. With any horse, the sending away process must be handled with care and sensitivity. Sending a wild or nervous horse away could make him more frightened and reinforce his desire to run away from humans. My advice is that you get him happy to be touched and leading before you think about Joining Up with him. After all, you will be using the same body language principles with all your contact with the horse, and will have plenty of opportunities to communicate in this way.

We now have to teach our wild horse that our touching and stroking him is a good thing and to teach him to lead a little. So how do we get to that stage?

TWO WAYS OF GETTING THE FIRST HEADCOLLAR ON

Rope on a Stick

The quickest way is to **put a rope straight over the horse's neck** so that you have the immediate advantage of being able to work with pressure and release. However, much depends on the individual horse and you must be prepared to spend whatever time is necessary whichever way you choose.

The main point here is that your attitude is so important. I am talking about the 'quickest way' but this 'quickest way' still includes working with the psychology of the horse and starting to educate him so he improves and is more confident for the next day. A common way of dealing with wild youngsters off the moors is to get them in a crush to worm, geld, vaccinate them, and trim their feet. You can even get a headcollar on them in there. Who knows how many bruises they sustain (at least you can see the cuts) and psychologically the whole traumatic experience can start up a fear of humans that lasts the rest of their lives.

Some of you may be practised 'lassoers' from your days as cowhands in Arizona; maybe not many of you though. Some of us less dextrous individuals have to go for rather less glamorous, yet equally practical methods. The rope on a stick method I am about to describe may not look as sexy as lassoing but has the advantage of being far easier, more reliable, and certainly less frightening for the horse if you set it up correctly. It is so easy it almost seems like 'cheating'. I can quite often work with a horse for less than fifteen minutes and in that time have the rope round his neck, start some stroking on his withers and neck, make the rope into a halter, start leading him in a few circles and then take the rope off and leave him.

The most extraordinary and rewarding thing is that the next time you go to see that horse, he is very likely to want to make contact with you. He will in fact, be at just the point of education where you left him. I have even had times when I have worked with youngsters just the once and when I returned six months later I could tell

photos 1–6: catching a horse with a rope

Putting a rope over their head with a stick

The 'catching area' will ideally be square or rectangular rather than round as the corners will be helpful to keep the horse still. You will also need a strong stick, with no rough edges or sharp points, about six to eight feet (two to two-and-a-half metres) long, with a fork at one end and a rope between twelve and twenty feet (four to six metres) in length with a ring fixed at one end. Arrange the rope on to the stick in such a way that you can place the loop over the horse's head and then pull the stick away in just one nifty move.

straightaway the ones I had worked with by their friendliness and confidence.

To make the catching with a stick manoeuvre even easier and to start getting him used to handling at the same time, you could initially start stroking him with the stick. A bamboo cane works very well. Not only is it light but it has convenient ridges, which are useful for scratching the horse's withers, mimicking what another horse might do. You really want a situation where the horse cannot get out of the stick's reach, so that even if he rushes about the stick stays with him. As soon as the horse stops for a moment, extremely gently move the stick away as a reward for the horse. See if you can gradually get to stroke the top of his neck with the stick. Then as previously suggested see if he will let you gently scratch his withers with the stick. If you can get him used to this he will be less concerned when you come to drop the rope over his neck. It is easier to take the loop of the rope

Touching the horse with a stick

down over his head, rather than trying to go up and over his nose, where he might see it coming and dodge it.

Once you have the rope around his neck, you can start to control the horse's movement a little.

Remember... horses' only way of showing leadership in the herd is by controlling other horses' movements. You only have to move the horse a very little for his whole attitude to change towards you. The easiest way to move the horse is to have the rope at a right angle to the length of the horse's body. You should be holding the rope at least nine feet (three metres) from the loop around the neck, as the greater length gives you more leverage, which puts you at an advantage. The higher up the horse's neck the rope is, the more influence you will have. If it is around the base of his neck it is ideally placed for him to tow you! This is where the fork in the end of the stick comes in handy, as

you can use it to ease the rope up the neck. Just squeeze on the rope a couple of times to give the horse notice that you are going to ask for something more. Then give a strong pull on the rope so the horse is unbalanced and has to take a step towards you. Immediately release the pressure, totally relax yourself, and give the horse a moment to take in what has happened.

It is easier for you if the horse is positioned in a corner so he has nowhere to pull away to. If he does try to pull away, the time when you are 'strongest' is just when either of his forelegs is off the ground as he goes to swing around. You are at an advantage then to give a pull and bring him round to face you. Again release the pressure of the rope and give the horse a minute or so to think. After you have given two or three of these pulls and got the horse to view his situation altogether differently, you can gently proceed to put a headcollar on the horse using much the same system as described in 'Advance and Retreat' on page 16. Don't rush the process, and only use the rope again if he goes to pull away.

It is easier if the horse is positioned in a corner

You don't get extra points for making life harder than it need be

At a demonstration I was brought a pony whose owner was very distressed and told the audience, as she had told me on the phone previously, that the pony would have to be put down if nothing could be done on the evening. The pony had been with the owner for four years and in that time she had never been able to get near enough to put a head-collar on. She felt it wasn't fair on him to keep him alive, as he had no quality of life if he couldn't accept human contact at all. He had been bought at the same sales as another pony who had progressed really well and was now being ridden. The 'easy' pony had been used as a lead horse to tempt our 'difficult' pony into the trailer.

The owner was concerned about how much we would charge for helping her at the demonstration When we said 'on the contrary we give you two free tickets as a reward for bringing him' she could not believe her luck! Interestingly this little pony had originally been accepted for another horsemanship demonstration but the organiser of the demonstration had rung back and said they couldn't take him after all because 'it would be impossible to do anything with him in the time slot of half an hour'. They offered to come back and help for £500 for the day! This had devastated the owner who by now was getting more and more desperate.

I showed the audience how he would not let me get near enough to touch him. You could get within about three feet (one metre) and then he would start to run off. He had obviously become well practiced at this and his owner must have had unending patience with him as she had tried over and over again. All that had happened in this case was that the pony had learned better and better all the ways not to be caught. I think the audience must have been thinking 'Oh my goodness this is going to be a long night!' Then the Intelligent Horsemanship Team immediately made the round pen into a smaller square shape, I brought out my stick and rope, and placed the rope over his neck in one move. This pony was a gift to do because the owner had not frightened him or done any harm at all. It was just that she had not been able to take that crucial move of getting the head-collar on. The pony's whole problem had been the anticipation of what might happen to him when he was caught. Being presented with his worst fear like this, and realising that it didn't hurt him at all, must have been such a relief to him. After that, progress was very easy. He could be led and handled with no problems and he even led nicely into the trailer within fifteen minutes of my first laying eyes on him. There would be no reason why the owner couldn't go on with him without any problems at all. I hope you appreciate the fact that this book is worth £500!

Advance and Retreat

If the youngster is settled and much more ready for human contact, rather than using the rope I might use the 'advance and retreat' method to get closer to him. As I approach him in the barn, I obviously would prefer him to face me, so if he is facing away at all I would square up to him a little i.e. outstretch my arms, look him in the eye, maybe even scuffle my feet a little until he moves round and positions himself to look at me. The instant he does this I drop my arms and eye contact, put my shoulders at a forty-five degree angle to him and move away from him. Moving away is the best reward for the youngster at this stage. Remember, the same dynamics exist in the early stages of any relationship, you 'make a move forward' to let it be known you want to be friends, but then you need to 'take a step back' and give that person some space to let them make the decision that they want to be close to you as well.

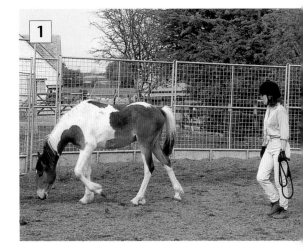

If he moves around you need to repeat the same procedure so that he finds it a little uncomfortable, through your body language, to move away from the position where you find it best to work with him. You want him to find that place as his comfort zone. If the horse is friendly to you, you keep your very 'friendly' body position to him. If he is unfriendly you use the 'unfriendly' body positioning until he turns round. Be sure to be consistent with this. You get some people who move gingerly around, quietly going 'there, there good boy' when the horse has its bottom turned towards them, but if the horse is turned facing them they immediately make a grab at his head. You can see how some horses get inadvertently trained to have their bottoms facing towards the stable door!

photos 1–5: the 'advance and retreat' method

with his nose. Sometimes they are so surprised by their bravery they jump back in horror!

The biggest mistake I see is people moving too quickly. Keep all your actions really smooth. Imagine your body is covered in heavy weights so you can't move anything quickly. Keep your breathing slow. I was trained by a hypnotherapist to concentrate on breathing out very slowly if I was nervous at all (of course, you will need to remember to breath in as well – but then generally nature sees to that). Giving a sigh or a yawn can help, horses will often mimic you and if they feel you are relaxed they will be more inclined to relax as well. (See 'Mirroring' in *Catching Horses Made Easy* in this series.)

Let him get used to the sound of your voice – but don't expect him to know what you are saying! Keep your voice low and calm. If you are nervous and start squeaking along in a high pitched voice it is going to do nothing to reassure your horse.

When I am working with a youngster in this way, I find it works well to go in for four or five short visits every day, getting a little bit closer each time, and rewarding him by going away

If he stays in his comfort zone, work at gradually getting closer to him. Each time he allows you to get a little bit closer, reward him again by moving away. You will find a curious thing happening, he will be 'drawn' to you and you will even see him take a step or two towards you each time you move away.

The next step is to allow him to sniff your hand. This is mimicking how two horses sniff each other. Put the back of your hand out gently (the back is less threatening than the front) and the youngster will often reach out and touch it

The horse reaching out to touch my hand

again. Soon he will be looking forward to your visits! Then you can gradually work on touching more areas; his shoulder, neck, mane and withers are generally the easiest to get to. He will soon find he enjoys a little scratch on the withers or in the mane, and once he lets you get that far, it is the start of a whole new relationship.

A note about unhandled horses

Never stand directly in front of an un-handled horse in these early stages. An unhandled youngster may strike out with a front leg as an instinctive protection. He is not being 'naughty' – he is just frightened. If he does strike out there is no need for you to do anything (except avoid it). As soon as you gain his confidence and trust he won't think about doing this again.

Interestingly, I have never known a totally unhandled youngster deliberately go to kick at a human. I believe this is a learned behaviour, taught as a result of humans hitting or aggravating them from behind. The time you may be in danger is if you are in a group of horses and one goes to kick out at another horse.

A note on the headcollar

This needs to be breakable, particularly if you are going to leave it on for any length of time. You may have to ask your saddler to make you up something specially if they are not available commercially in your area.

Once he is comfortable with you stroking his neck the next step is to start stroking his neck whilst you are holding a headcollar that opens both over the head and over the nose. Gradually get your horse used to the headcollar and then 'feed' it over his neck so it can be done up. Then gently edge it forward to do up over his nose. You need to be gentle and tactful, though firm enough so that if he goes to move away you can stay with him if the opportunity is there. Make sure you do not get into any sort of battle with him – skiing around clinging onto his neck is unlikely to do either of you any good! Once you have done this relax and come out of the stable and take a break for a few minutes. Let him take in the fact that he is now a 'domesticated' animal!

If the unhandled youngster is obviously quite friendly and confident then it will be an easy decision to go for the advance and retreat method. If he is very wild and there is less time available you may be better to go for the rope on a stick method. Sometimes it is hard to be quite sure of which is the best way to proceed. You may go in to touch him a few times and he turns out to be more nervous than you originally thought and then it's perfectly all right to change your mind. Keep your ego out of the equation. Just keep in mind 'What is the best thing for this horse right now?' There are the options we have already discussed and then as you proceed you might ask yourself 'Do I need to change what I'm doing?' 'Would this horse and I be better if we got help from a more experienced person at this stage?' Intelligent Horsemanship is all about being able to ask yourself honest questions and give yourself honest answers.

photos 1–6: putting a headcollar on

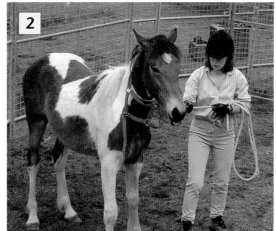

ESTABLISHING TRUST

Once we have our 'wild' horse in a headcollar and in an enclosed area we are pretty much in the same position as the person who has a very nervous horse which cannot be caught. I have known horses which could be ridden but not caught, even in the stable. It may be that they have just received insufficient education and handling from the ground, or it may be, sadly, that these horses have been beaten by someone on the ground, and so have a well-founded fear of human beings. This is often the case with some of the 'rescue' horses we deal with.

It may be a good idea to leave the breakable headcollar on during the day for the first couple of days so it is easy to go in and make contact with your horse every now and then. Do not go in and get hold of the headcollar directly as it could be dangerous if the horse pulls back. Clip your rope onto the back of the headcollar in a gentle and easy movement and then start to stroke your horse.

Before we can turn our wild or nervous horse out in a field and catch him easily we need to establish a total trust with him in the stable or enclosed area. We need this horse to be happy with us touching him all over his body. This is a gradual process of desensitisation for the horse. First of all find the areas he is happy with you touching (it may only be his wither), and then gradually work out into the areas he's more concerned about.

Remember...

1. **A horse must be calm in order to learn anything.** It is really important, as with all the exercises, to approach the horse in a relaxed, non-adversarial manner.

2. **Horses have to learn to be lead, it is not natural to them. Their natural reaction is to pull against pressure.** You can start giving your horse some lessons in leading now. (See *Leading and Loading*.) Do not hold the rope short, have about three feet (one metre) of slack in the rope. Avoid a situation where you are struggling and keep a very elastic pressure on the rope. Only lead the horse in small circles to start with – going one step at a time. You 'ask' by putting a little elastic pressure on the rope. As you are attempting initially to move the horse at quite an acute angle it will be hard for him to avoid taking a step as you are in effect, unbalancing him a little. When he moves you release the pressure immediately, and so 'reward' him. Do two or three circles in each direction. If at the

photos 1–3: first leading: horses may resist strongly the first time they feel the slightest pressure

same time you make a 'kissing' noise (not 'clicking' which is designed to 'gee' horses up) you will find that if you undo the rope and continue to walk round him making the kissing noise, he will very likely still follow you. This is your early stages of 'follow up'.

You also want him to accept you touching him all over, eventually even his ears, inside his mouth, on his tail and lower legs, but that will come with time. To start with, just concentrate on him happily accepting you touching the main areas of his body. If you have any worries about touching a particular area use an artificial hand until you are happy he is relaxed enough for you to move in closer in safety. Never force the issue, just do a little more each time until he gradually feels more comfort-

able with you. If the horse does not like to be touched and moves around try and stay with him (easier with the long hand) and then move away the moment he stands quietly. This is your way of rewarding him. 'You see, if you stand still, I move away.'

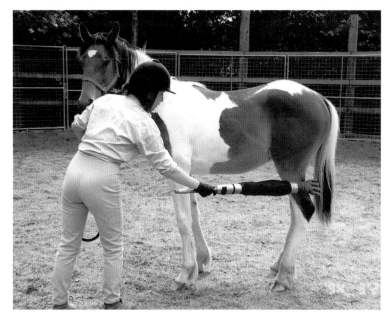

A horse should stand quietly, and soon grow to greatly enjoy you stroking him all over. They will learn to appreciate a 'lovely rub' on the front of their face, just between the eyes. The shiatsu practitioners call this 'the third eye', and it is meant to have special properties. Maybe it is soothing because it is so close to the brain; it could be the reason people pay so much for facials. I mean, we don't seriously imagine we are going to come out looking like Cameron Diaz do we? I believe it is also well worth learning the massage techniques as recommended by Linda Tellington-Jones or Mary Bromiley. As well as the physiological benefits it also encourages us to spend additional quality time with our horses which can only be a good thing.

photos 1–7: **going back to the barn or stable**